In the year 2036, the US Government revealed there were other lifeforms in the galaxy, and they were not friendly. However, they also had some good news: a company known as the Blue Haven Corporation had built an army of androids to defend the world.

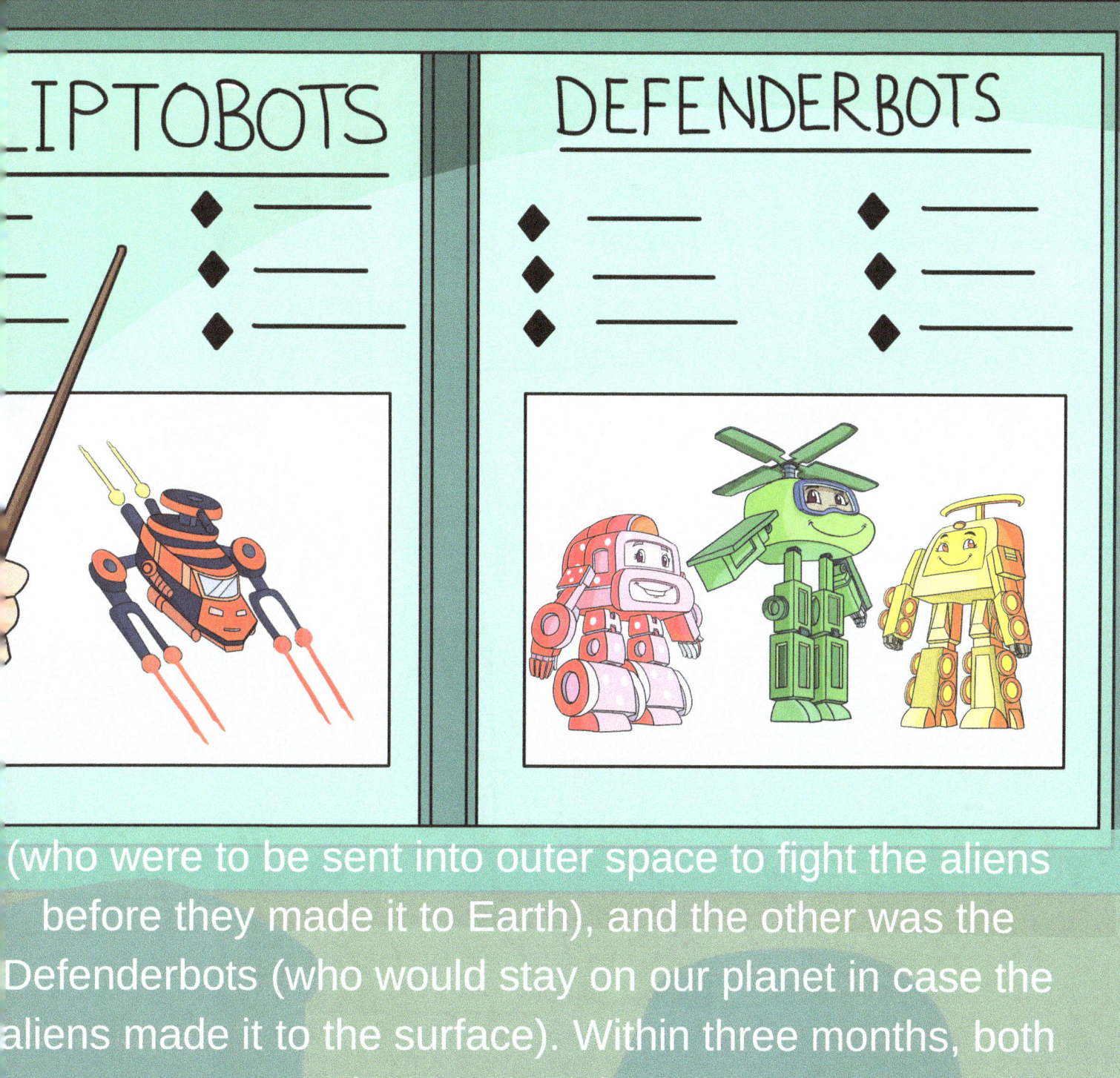

(who were to be sent into outer space to fight the aliens before they made it to Earth), and the other was the Defenderbots (who would stay on our planet in case the aliens made it to the surface). Within three months, both armies were ready to fight.

Since they were more concerned with the preservation of life, the Defenderbots Prototypes were programmed with strong moral character.

DEFENDERBOTS

The Eliptobots had been created to destroy the aliens, so they had no such programming.

ELIPTO BOTS

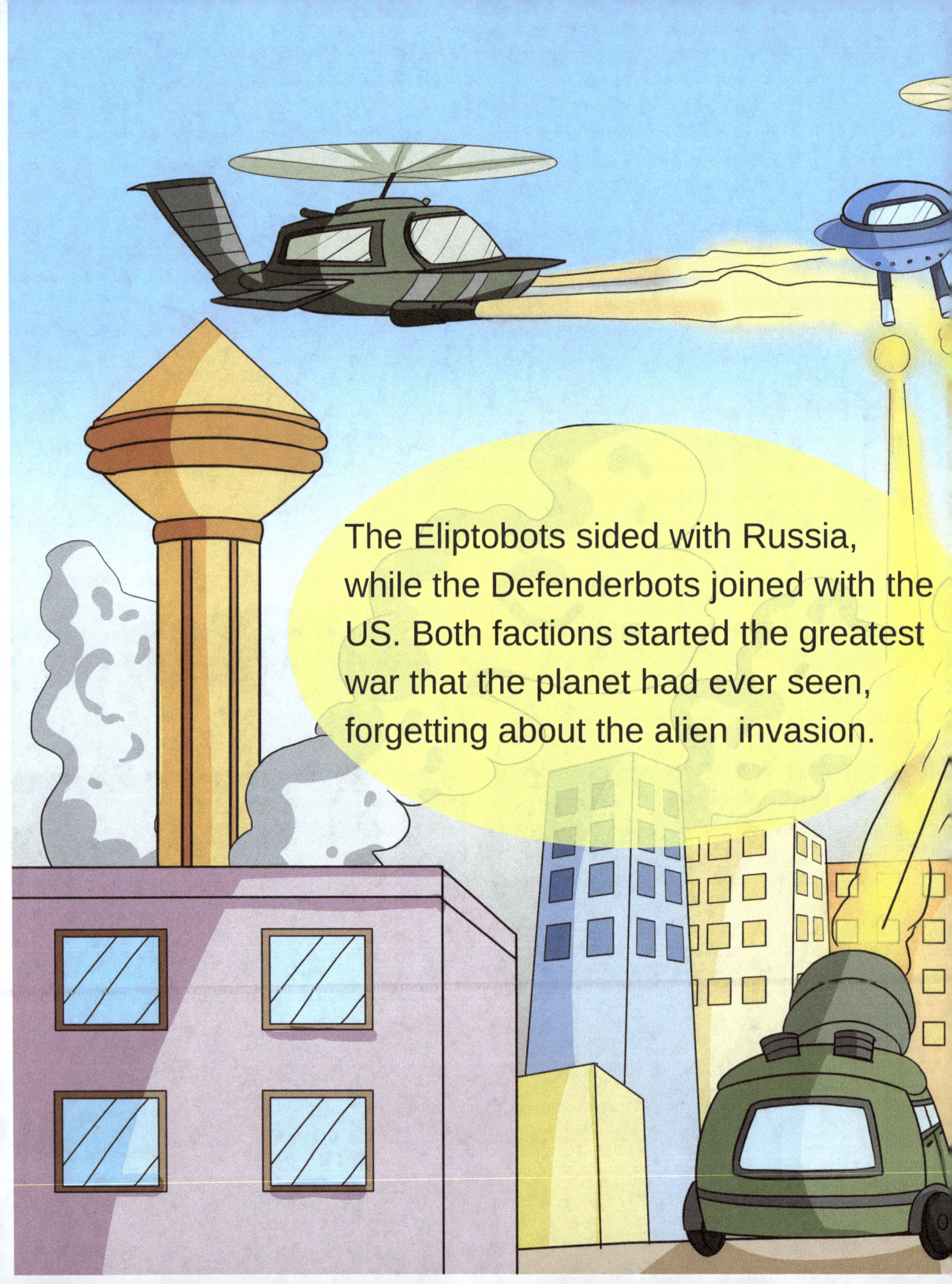

The Eliptobots could fly, which allowed them to drop bombs on their enemies. Defenderbots had the ability to use electrically generated force fields and rocket launchers.

Eventually the alien space crafts came to Earth and attacked every major city.

At first, each side thought it was the other using new weaponry. Soon they realized it was the aliens. The leaders of the warring nations got together and called a truce.

At first the androids faced defeat. Then the Blue Haven Corporation updated the androids: Sun, Ladybug, and Eve.

www.ingramcontent.com/pod-product-compliance
Lightning Source LLC
Chambersburg PA
CBHW081400080526
44588CB00016B/2564